Kathaine

the
REALLY
really
BUSY PERSON'S
book on
MARRIAGE

To the friends and supporters of Care for the Family – you are changing lives. Thank You!

the
REALLY
really
BUSY PERSON'S
book on
MARRIAGE

Rob Parsons & Katharine Hill

Muddy
Pearl

First published in 2016 by Muddy Pearl, Edinburgh, Scotland.

www.muddypearl.com
books@muddypearl.com

© Care for the Family

Cartoons © David McNeill 2016

Rob Parsons and Katharine Hill have asserted their right under the Copyright, Designs and Patents Act, 1988 to be identified as the authors of this work.

Scripture quotations are taken from
The Holy Bible, New International Version (Anglicised), NIV®.
Copyright © 1979, 1984, 2011 Biblica, Inc., formerly International Bible Society.
Used by permission of Hodder & Stoughton Publishers, an Hachette UK company.
All rights reserved worldwide.
"New International Version" and "NIV" are registered trademarks of Biblica, Inc.
UK trademark number 1448790.

British Library Cataloguing in Publication Data.
A catalogue record for this book is available from the British Library

ISBN 978-1-910012-30-7

Typeset and designed by RevoCreative. www.revocreative.co.uk

Printed and bound in Great Britain by Bell and Bain Ltd, Glasgow

ACKNOWLEDGMENTS

Thanks once again go to our whole team at Care for the Family. Our Senior Editor, Sheron Rice, has done an absolutely brilliant job again (we can't think of doing a book without her!), and we are so grateful to David McNeill for his wonderful cartoons. Many thanks, finally, to our publishers, Stephanie and Richard Heald of Muddy Pearl – we love working with you.

For almost thirty years we have been writing and speaking about family issues: over twenty books written and a million people spoken to at live events in cultures as diverse as Borneo and Bournemouth. A year ago we wrote our first book together – The Really, Really Busy Person's Book on Parenting. The response to that little book was overwhelming, and we had so much fun writing it that as soon as the ink was dry we turned our minds to the next big topic. It is one that we have written and spoken about so much over the years: marriage.

In the work we do we see lots of fun and joy in relationships, but we also see a lot of pain. We know there are no easy answers to the traumas that hit many of our marriages, but we also know that down-to-earth, practical help can be revolutionary in strengthening and even repairing relationships.

So here's the next book in the series. It's our very best shot at bringing together the essence of what we've written on marriage and wisdom from around the world, and includes, of course, David McNeill's brilliant cartoons!

This is a book to dip into, to bring a smile, and perhaps even restore a little hope. Keep it in the car, on your desk, in the kitchen, by your bed or anywhere at all where you can catch an odd minute to read a page or two – even if you're a really really busy person!

We hope you enjoy it.

Rob and Katharine

The greatest thing in life is to find
somebody, somewhere, who will love us...
anyway.

SUCCESS IN MARRIAGE IS MORE THAN FINDING THE RIGHT PERSON. IT IS ABOUT *BEING* THE RIGHT PERSON.

Real communication is vital if relationships are to deepen and grow, and yet there are so many couples who have never known it. They returned from honeymoon all those years ago, the phone started to ring, there was the house to fix up, so many friends to invite around, and then the children came along. They will sometimes look at those children, now teenagers, and say, 'Where have the years gone? They've flown by.' What they do not yet realise is the void that is at the heart of their marriage. Life with the children, and the sheer busyness of the everyday, keeps them, even saves them, from thinking about their relationship. But the day may come when the children leave, and other activities stop, and they will sit in a room, look at each other, and say in their hearts, 'Who are you?'

If I get married, I want to be very married.

— AUDREY HEPBURN

The silliest line in any film ever is found in the old blockbuster *Love Story*: 'Love means never having to say you're sorry.' Actually, the opposite is true: 'Love means always having to say you're sorry.'

Forgiveness is not brushing the hurt under
the carpet and pretending it doesn't matter.
It involves confronting the ways you may
have hurt each other, bringing them out
into the open and then, for the sake of the
relationship, choosing to let go.

At the heart of marriage is a little word that packs a big punch: *sacrifice*.

As wonderful as the feeling of love is, it is not enough for a marriage. There will be many different times when we need to decide to love – even when we don't feel like it: turning off our favourite TV programme when we know our partner needs to talk or doing that hated chore when it's not our turn ... it's the stuff of commitment.

My grandchildren love to go into our loft. And when Lily (aged five) and I were up there the other day, she discovered an old box filled with Valentine's Day cards that Dianne and I had sent to each other when we were teenagers. (We were aged thirteen on our first date!) Some have the letters 'SWALK' scrawled on the envelope – a little acronym that first appeared on letters sent home in the Second World War – 'Sealed with a loving kiss'. Another had 'BOLTOP' written on it – 'Better on lips than on paper'!

A five-year-old finger traced the shape of the red heart on one card and asked, "Was Nandi your girlfriend, Pops?"

"She still is!" I say.

Little eyes grew wide.

When we got married, an old couple gave us some advice that they got from the Bible: 'Let not the sun go down on your wrath.'

A few years later someone told us a more modern translation and it has stayed with us: 'Resolve the flak before you hit the sack.'

In her book *The Best Kept Secret*, psychologist Janet Reibstein looks at what it takes to sustain love during marriage. 'A lifetime of love,' she says, 'can mean an awfully long time.' She has found that couples who keep their love alive do so by connecting together and enjoying each other's company. 'From sharing books, theatre, music and travel, to sport, gardening and mutual friends, these couples spend a good proportion of their lives finding fun and pleasure together. They have a shared sense of humour, built up over shared experiences.'

Whether couples have been married for two months or twenty years, it can often be the little things that make a difference. Small, everyday points of connection over time can weave themselves into the very fabric of the marriage.

Janet Reibstein, *The Best Kept Secret:
How love can last forever Bloomsbury,* 2007.

HOW **NOT** TO HANDLE CONFLICT

— Forget the issue and attack the person

Sue asked her husband, Mike, to pick up some milk on the way home. An hour later, he walks through the door – his hands empty. 'You forgot again, didn't you?' she says.

If she left it there they could have an argument about why he forgot, but she decides to abandon the issue and attack Mike himself: 'You're totally useless – a complete waste of space.' The second it's out of her mouth she knows what she has done – but even then she doesn't know its long-term effect. He may never forget those words and the way they made him feel that day.

On her golden wedding anniversary, my grandmother revealed the secret of her long and happy marriage. 'On my wedding day, I decided to choose ten of my husband's faults which, for the sake of our marriage, I would overlook,' she explained. A guest asked her to name some of the faults. 'To tell the truth,' she replied, 'I never did get around to listing them. But whenever my husband did something that made me hopping mad, I would say to myself, "Lucky for him that's one of the ten."'

There are marriages of twenty years, and in all that time the partners have not had twenty minutes when they have sat in a quiet room and actually listened to each other. Not twenty minutes in twenty years.

WHEN YOU GET HOME, TRY TO SPEAK TO YOUR PARTNER BEFORE DOING ANYTHING ELSE.

When love dies, so often the real cause is not the most obvious one. Not every marriage that I have seen break up has had incredible conflict in it; not everyone has known sexual difficulties or an affair. No, the real killer is often hidden. It is simply that the couple has stopped talking to each other.

Lack of communication doesn't mean not talking about anything. It means not talking about anything that *matters*. There comes a point in many marriages where one of the partners either cannot or will not discuss issues that are vital to the other.

EAT A MEAL BY CANDLELIGHT OCCASIONALLY.

When you fall in love it is a temporary madness. It erupts like an earthquake, and then it subsides. And when it subsides, you have to make a decision. You have to work out whether your roots are to become so entwined together that it is inconceivable that you should ever part. Because this is what love is. Love is not breathlessness, it is not excitement … It is not lying awake at night imagining that he is kissing every part of your body … For that is just being in love, which any of us can convince ourselves we are. Love itself is what is left over when being in love has burned away.

– LOUIS DE BERNIERES, *CAPTAIN CORELLI'S MANDOLIN*

LAUGH MORE TOGETHER.

Talk to each other about money issues.
People in marriages that break up often say
that financial trouble was the major problem.

Sarah and Neil had been married for just over six years and had a daughter, Samantha, aged three. Samantha's bedroom was being redecorated, which meant that she was tucked up on a mattress at the foot of her parents' bed.

It was a Thursday, and Sarah and Neil kept Thursday evenings for themselves – their 'date night'. By the time they'd got Samantha to bed it was eight o'clock. They'd lit candles, devoured an enormous pizza, and watched *Sleepless in Seattle* on DVD (again!). At just gone midnight they crept into a pitch-black bedroom and slid quietly into bed.

It was then that Neil decided to move across the bed towards his wife.

'Don't even think about it,' Sarah said.

'But, darling, Samantha's fast asleep.'

'No!'

'Sarah, don't do this to me.'

'Neil – our daughter is asleep in our room. No!'

'Darling ... please.'

It was at this point when another voice joined the conversation. It seemed to come from the foot of the bed. 'Daddy! When Mummy says, "No" she means "No"!'

A marriage does not normally die overnight. So often it is that week by week, month by month, year upon year, the couple simply grow apart. One couple describe it as 'a creeping separateness'.

The antidote to 'a creeping separateness'
is not usually found in expensive holidays,
or what some have called 'quality time', but
in quite a lot of 'ordinary time' spent doing
everyday things together.

I'm no good at DIY but some years ago I needed to trim the bottom of a door after a carpet had been laid. I borrowed an electric saw, which went absolutely berserk every time I switched it on. My wife was holding the door as I tried to perform this tricky operation and before long we were yelling at each other. Finally, after coming incredibly near to severing one of her legs, the job was done, but by now a row was in full swing. It was only when we saw that I'd taken far too much off the bottom of the door that we started laughing. 'At least we won't have to get up to let the cat in!' my wife said. We collapsed in hysterics but it could have been so different.

Take a trip down memory lane: have an
evening with your old photographs.

If we laugh at ourselves, there is great hope for us. One couple have named their great fights – it helps them remember not to repeat them, and also to realise how silly some were. Among the top ten are: 'The Battle of the Christmas Turkey,' 'The Skirmish at Debenham's Lingerie Counter,' and 'High Noon at Gatwick Airport.'

There is no shortage of time-saving devices, fast food and digital calendars that allow us to plan every minute of the day. The only thing we don't have any more of is time. But none of us would live like this if we thought that life would always be this busy and we would never have time to build good relationships with our husband, wife or children. And so we fool ourselves that this is a busy period of our lives and that, when it is over, we will have more time. We wait patiently, but the slower day never comes.

He used to say he didn't have time for us because he was working so hard for our sake. I told him hundreds of times we'd have preferred less things and more of him.

Put on love.

– ST PAUL

TRY TO HAVE AN EVENING ONCE A
WEEK FOR JUST THE TWO OF YOU.
DEFEND IT WITH YOUR LIFE.

HOW **NOT** TO HANDLE CONFLICT

– Never lose an argument

There is nothing more certain to create terminal conflict in a marriage than one of the partners being brilliant with words. These creatures always have the final say. They have the ability to twist, manipulate, quote expert authority and generally make you wish you hadn't bothered to start this particular fight. And they really believe they win arguments. What they don't see is what they leave behind – the unresolved anger, the bitterness inside, and a growing resentment at not being able to put your position.

There is only one hope for such a person. They must learn to *lose* arguments; to understand that winning is normally nothing like as important as it appears to be; to back off a little and give the other person space to say what they feel. When they do, they discover two things. First: conflict gets resolved faster. Second: the day after, they can't even remember what the row was about.

Husband: My sex life is like my Ferrari.

Wife: But you haven't got a Ferrari.

Husband: Mmmm...

Let your children see that you
respect your partner.

Continuing to love each other is a choice. The reality is that none of us knows what the future will bring. When you promise to love your husband or wife for better or for worse, you are choosing to put their needs before yours. You are committing yourselves to them, to seek always what is best for them. This runs counter to culture in today's me-centred society, but it is the only way to work together to create a marriage that lasts a lifetime.

BE THE FIRST TO SAY SORRY.

Forgiveness feels pain but doesn't hoard it; it allows tomorrow to break free of yesterday. It is always hard, sometimes foolish and, at its heart, God-like.

When we hit tough times in our relationship it is important to realise that we're not alone. We're not the only couple in the world who are suddenly finding it hard to talk together, we're not the only ones in financial trouble, and there are others whose sex life isn't always 'absolutely fabulous'! When we realise that it's not just us, it takes the pressure off and we can more easily find a way through.

Before starting an argument, ask yourself:
'Is this worth fighting over?'

How would you make a marriage work?

'Tell your wife that she looks pretty, even if she looks like a truck.'

– RICKY, AGE 10

What many people crave is not somebody to talk to them but somebody who will actually *listen*.

Love is a force more formidable than any other. It is invisible – it cannot be seen or measured, yet it is powerful enough to transform you in a moment, and offer you more joy than any material possession could.

- BARBARA DE ANGELIS

It's important to make time for your children, but it's even more vital to make time for each other. The best thing you can do for your children is to invest in your marriage.

I was nine years old when my dad took me to the circus and I saw him – the spinning plate man. I watched wide-eyed as he went through his act. First, he took just one plate, put it on a pole, spun it and, hey presto, it stayed up. I would have clapped just for that, but he had greater ideas. He had fifty plates, and he put them all on poles and got them all spinning. Brilliant!

What I didn't know, as a small boy of nine, was that it was only possible for three minutes. If, at the end of his show, we'd yelled, 'Do it again, do it again!', he would have rushed from plate to plate as he tried to do what we wanted, but soon the plates would have begun to fall and he'd stumble as he tried so hard to keep them all going... forever. And, finally, if we'd yelled, 'Do it again! Do it again!' enough times, he would have collapsed amongst the shattered plates.

HOLD HANDS MORE OFTEN.

When one parent becomes obsessed with a child to the exclusion of their partner, the marriage begins to operate as though there's an affair going on. And there is.

A good sexual relationship doesn't start in the bedroom. If a man is more interested in the sports page than discussing issues that matter to his wife, then he had better take the sports page to bed – he's going to have plenty of time to read it. That's why the old advice is true: 'If a man wants a wild Friday night, he had better begin working on it on Monday morning.'

I remember a Saturday afternoon, soon after we were first married. It was a beautiful summer's day and we were strolling along a pier. We were young, happy and had our married lives in front of us. Just ahead, an elderly couple were walking together. They were grey-haired and stooped. They held each other's hands, and he leant slightly on his wife for support. They seemed to us like two weathered trees that had huddled together through some hard winters over the years and then forgotten to separate again. We giggled and I said, "One day we'll be like that!" Dianne said, "I hope so."

Not long ago, over forty years later, we walked along a different pier on another sunny day. Dianne had her arm in mine and leant on me a little for support. She had just had her second hip replacement. We ambled along, and suddenly I heard a gentle giggle just behind us.

The young couple were hand in hand, and of course I don't really know what was amusing them so much.

But I have a clue ...

It takes faith to engage in conflict — faith that you're both committed to this relationship and so can afford to positively work through tension and disagreement without fear that one of you will walk away.

HOW **NOT** TO HANDLE CONFLICT

– Bring out the old mortar bombs

Every marriage has at least six of these hidden away. We bring them out when our back is against the wall and we need some heavy weaponry. They could involve sex, DIY, weight, the way we discipline or don't discipline the children. Typical classics will draw on past events with in-laws, holidays, and money. Sometimes we feel ashamed of using them because they are so old, so we preface them with, "You always ..." or "You never ..." Other phrases that freshen them up a little are, "I'll never forget when ..." or "The problem with you is that you are still ..."

The real disadvantage in using old mortar bombs is they don't allow for change, or that somebody may be sorry about the past. Lay them down – if only to find new ones!

THE REALLY REALLY BUSY PERSON'S...

Forgiveness is hard. You don't realise what a
good memory you've got until you try with
all your heart to forget something.

I remember at the end of a seminar a young couple waiting patiently to speak with me. They held back until they were sure the auditorium was empty and then he told me his story. He had an affair the year before. He said, 'I told my wife what I had done, and I asked for her forgiveness. I took my wedding ring off and said, "Don't put that back on my finger until you can trust me again."' And then he smiled, lifted his hand and said, 'Last month she put it back on my finger.'

He was relieved, but I turned to see how she was reacting. Her head was bowed. I said to him, 'Forgive me if I'm wrong, but I think when she put that ring back on your finger she was not saying, "I trust you again." She was saying, "With all my heart I want to trust you again."' She raised her head and said, 'That's how I feel.'

If we are to have a good sexual relationship, one of the prerequisites is that we stop taking ourselves so seriously and imagining that our sex lives are going to impress Hollywood. In that particular suburb of Los Angeles, it seems that the sex is always wonderful. The beds are always made, and the women look fantastic and seem to have an insatiable appetite for love-making. The men are animal-like and yet tender and never fall asleep straight afterwards. The real world is a little different. In the real world there are periods, mind-numbing tiredness, and children who are pre-timed to wake at the very hint of passion. Enjoy the films, but don't compare your love-life to them.

Give your wife flowers when it's not
your anniversary.

It's hard to have a decent row with somebody who always wins.

Although we have different needs, we can easily assume that our spouse's needs are the same as ours. We then get frustrated when our misdirected efforts to meet what we think are their needs do not have the desired effect.

WHEN WE'RE OUT SHOPPING
I WISH HE'D HOLD MY HAND
OCCASIONALLY INSTEAD OF
WALKING 100 YARDS IN FRONT.

THE REALLY REALLY BUSY PERSON'S...

There is nothing more infuriating than pouring out your heart to somebody, and suddenly realising that they're watching something that's going on behind you.

Use one of these starter questions to get you going in conversation:

- *If you could do anything, go anywhere, or be anyone, what would your choice be?*
- *What things in our marriage do you love most?*
- *If you could change one thing about yourself, what would it be?*
- *If you could change one thing about me, what would it be?*
- *What dreams do you have for your life and our family?*
- *What changes could we make to create more time for each other?*
- *If somebody suddenly left you £1000, what would you spend it on?*

How can a stranger tell if two people are married?

'You might have to guess, based on whether they seem to be yelling at the same kids.'

– DERRICK, AGE 8

Our sex life can so easily become the casualty of over-busy lives. We're just too shattered. For that reason, some couples have discovered that 'planning ahead' is not such a bad idea. 'I know it sounds a bit clinical, but life is so hectic we found that if we didn't plan ahead we were just too tired for sex. I'm not saying it will work for everybody, but we have come to regard these nights as special. Of course it can still happen spontaneously, but we're beginning to see the value of taking our sexual relationship seriously.'

I believe that often there are 'innocent' partners when it comes to affairs. I do not mean by this that they were the perfect husband or wife, or that there was nothing they couldn't have profitably changed about the way in which they related to their partner. I mean that they had done nothing to deserve their partner's affair.

The other man's grass may look greener...

but it still needs mowing.

We sow the seeds of tragedy when we want our partner to become someone they just can't be.

Often the very differences that may have attracted us to each other before we were married can be a source of irritation and conflict afterwards. When we first met we loved the fact that they were spontaneous ... now we think they are unpredictable; and whereas we used to think them strong ... now they seem so stubborn. Sometimes, we will have to accept and even celebrate our differences.

Don't confuse your partner's need for space
with rejection.

HOW **NOT** TO HANDLE CONFLICT

– Widen the issue

With this one, instead of just arguing over the situation in hand, we try to think of other unrelated events to give us a bit more firepower. It goes something like this: 'I can't believe you spent all that money on clothes – you always think of yourself first – you're so selfish,' and then, 'That's why last year's holiday with my mother was such a disaster.'

Now the fascinating thing is that the person who has this tactic used on them does not normally say, 'What on earth has last year's holiday with your mother got to do with my overspending?' No, they widen the argument as well, 'OK, I'm selfish. And you're so great you've been passed over for promotion four times.' The blue touch paper is now lit. Stand well back.

A successful marriage requires falling in love many times, always with the same person.

— MIGNON MCLAUGHLIN

Husband to wife as they arrive at a party:
'And don't try to stop me each time I say,
"Stop me if you've heard this before ..."'

Whenever you find families where relationships are strong, you always find the same ingredient: people encourage each other.

If the course of married life has seasons, then most begin in summer. They are days filled with warmth when we not only say we are in love, but we feel in love. Of course, to love in summer is relatively easy, but marriages that are to last have a much harder test ahead: it is the challenge of surviving the winter of our relationship. It is not always possible, but we will never know long term love with anybody unless, at least for a while, we can love in January.

I'm sure we chanted lots of rhymes in the playground when I was a child, but the very silliest must surely be, 'Sticks and stones may break my bones, but words will never hurt me.' If I could have discovered any lesson in life earlier, it would be to have understood the sheer power of the words we speak.

So if I could rewind the clock, I would pay more compliments instead of those silly carping criticisms I've sometimes been so fond of. When we went out I would say more often, 'You look great tonight,' instead of helpfully pointing out that 'Your hair looks funny.'

You can give without loving, but you can never love without giving. The great acts of love are done by those who are habitually performing small acts of kindness.

- VICTOR HUGO, *LES MISERABLES*

NEVER BRING YOUR PARTNER DOWN IN PUBLIC.

They aren't sure exactly when it happened, but after about five years of marriage Lizzie and Jeremy stopped eating meals together at the table and moved to having them on the sofa in front of the television. One day they realised that they had lost one of the main times when they used to really communicate together. Not every night, but most nights now, they try to eat with the television off and – they talk.

ZOOOM!

From the day your children are born get
ready for the day when they will leave. It can
happen so fast it will take your breath away.
Give them all that you can, but don't build
your lives solely around them.

BE BEST FRIENDS.

I think I have been to almost a hundred weddings and as I attended a recent one, the minister read words that I have heard time and time again. They seem to have lost none of their ancient power.

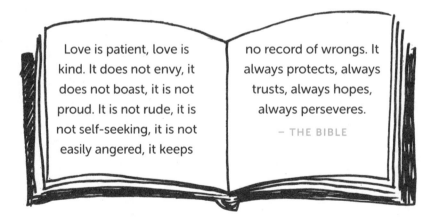

Love is patient, love is kind. It does not envy, it does not boast, it is not proud. It is not rude, it is not self-seeking, it is not easily angered, it keeps no record of wrongs. It always protects, always trusts, always hopes, always perseveres.

— THE BIBLE

Remember the sheer power of encouragement. It should never be insincere, but it can be for small things.

I have known many people who look at other couples and wish that their partner were more like their friend's. They whisper, 'If only Jim were more like Steve,' or, 'You're so lucky having Vicky.' Sometimes it is physical things that they want their partner to change. One of the saddest things I saw on television was a woman who was married to a plastic surgeon. In an effort to please her husband she had already had ten cosmetic operations on various parts of her body. She smiled confidently and said, 'He'll never leave me. If he gets tired of me he can change the way I look.'

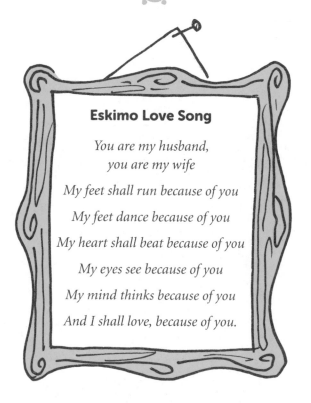

Eskimo Love Song

You are my husband,
you are my wife

My feet shall run because of you

My feet dance because of you

My heart shall beat because of you

My eyes see because of you

My mind thinks because of you

And I shall love, because of you.

There will come a time in every marriage when we love not 'because of' but 'in spite of' our feelings. It has at its heart not just the *feeling* of love, but the *will* to love.

CRITICISE LESS: DISCOVER THE POWER OF PRAISE.

Sometimes people say to me, 'But some marriages are surely over.' Well, perhaps they are, but don't ask me to tell you which ones. Over the years I have seen countless couples, whose marriages seemed to be dead, decide to fight to keep their family together – and some in that very process have found a love they thought was gone forever.

KEEP YOUR PROMISES.

Five ways to say I love you:

– Gary Chapman, *The 5 Love Languages*

THE REALLY REALLY BUSY PERSON'S...

I remember when you leaned in close to kiss me,
and I swear that not a single force on earth could
stop the trembling of my hand.

I was counselling a couple and as they spoke, each would bring the other down. The air was filled with vitriol. I interrupted them and asked the wife if she could see any good quality in her husband of which she was proud. She answered in a heartbeat: 'He's a brilliant dad.' I saw a look of amazement cross his face.

The atmosphere in the room changed in a moment and I slipped out and left them alone for a while. They had spent ten years bringing each other down, playing the dignity-destroying game of verbal volleyball. They were experiencing something written in the book of Proverbs by one of the wisest men who ever lived: 'The tongue has the power of life and death.' But it was not too late for them to discover the life-changing impact of praise.

*A woman marries a man with the ridiculous
notion that she can change him and he with the
foolish idea that she will be the same forever.*

KEEP SHORT
ACCOUNTS.

We imagine the kind of person who would make us completely happy. If only he or she were thinner or fatter or wittier or stronger with the children. We may think we want a partner who is attractive, humorous, good around the house, a brilliant cook or DIY specialist, and a sexual athlete. But the person we are married to cannot be all of those. And when we are consumed with the idea of the kind of person we want our husband or wife to be, we so often miss the person that they *are*.

Sometimes after a marriage is over, a partner will look back and wonder, 'Why were those things such a big deal to me, when he was kind, and always there for me?' or 'Why was her dress size so much more important to me than the person that she was?'

TAKE WALKS TOGETHER MORE OFTEN.

You know you are in love when the two of you can go grocery shopping together.

– WOODY HARRELSON

I believe that nothing comes close to the affair for having the ability so quickly and with such surgical skill to decimate families.

Part of the power of the affair is that you can impress someone new so very easily. If you want to impress your marriage partner, you have to do it over many years, but the affair can dazzle in a moment and seems to have the ability to make those involved suspend any rational thought. Husband, wife, children, friends, careers – they all count for little in the light of this new relationship. It enables those involved to forget all the hard lessons learnt, and it whispers in their ears, 'It will be different with me.'

THE WAY TO LOVE ANYTHING IS TO REALISE IT MIGHT BE LOST FOREVER.

AND SUDDENLY, ALL OF THE LOVE SONGS WERE ABOUT YOU.

If I could do it over again, this is what I'd do:

- *I would laugh more – at our mistakes and our joys.*

- *I would listen more.*

- *I would be more honest about my own weaknesses, never pretending perfection.*

- *Instead of focusing on my partner's shortcomings, I'd focus on mine.*

- *I would encourage more and give more praise.*

- *I would pay more attention to little things, like acts of kindness and words of thoughtfulness.*

'Two are better than one … if either of them falls down, one can help the other up.'

– THE BIBLE

I shall do one thing in this life – one thing certain – and that is, love you, and long for you, and keep wanting you till I die.

THOMAS HARDY,

FAR FROM THE MADDING CROWD

Grow old with me! The best is yet to be.

ROBERT BROWNING

Care for the Family is a national charity which aims to promote strong family life and help those who face family difficulties. Working throughout the UK and the Isle of Man, we provide parenting, relationship and bereavement support through our events, courses, training and other resources. For more information, and to explore our wide range of resources on all aspects of family life, visit our website at **www.careforthefamily.org.uk**